Let's DRAW!

BIRDS AND BUTTERFLIES

How2DrawAnimals

Brimming with creative inspiration, how-to projects, and useful information to enrich your everyday life, quarto.com is a favorite destination for those pursuing their interests and passions.

© 2022 Quarto Publishing Group USA Inc.
Illustrations and text © 2022 P. Mendoza

First published in 2022 by Walter Foster Jr., an imprint of The Quarto Group.
100 Cummings Center, Suite 265D, Beverly, MA 01915, USA.
T (978) 282-9590 F (978) 283-2742 **www.quarto.com** • **www.walterfoster.com**

Walter Foster Jr. titles are also available at discount for retail, wholesale, promotional, and bulk purchase. For details, contact the Special Sales Manager by email at specialsales@quarto.com or by mail at The Quarto Group, Attn: Special Sales Manager, 100 Cummings Center, Suite 265D, Beverly, MA 01915, USA.

ISBN: 978-0-7603-8078-9

Digital edition published in 2022
eISBN: 978-0-7603-8079-6

10 9 8 7 6 5 4 3 2

TABLE OF CONTENTS

TOOLS & MATERIALS

Welcome! You don't need much to start learning how to draw. Anyone can draw with just a pencil and piece of scrap paper, but if you want to get more serious about your art, additional artist's supplies are available.

PAPER If you choose printer paper, buy a premium paper that is thick enough and bright. Portable sketch pads keep all your drawings in one place, which is convenient. For more detailed art pieces, use a fine art paper.

PENCILS Standard No. 2 pencils and mechanical pencils are great to start with and inexpensive. Pencils with different graphite grades can be very helpful when shading because a specific grade (such as 4H, 2B, or HB) will only get so dark.

PENCIL SHARPENER Electric sharpeners are faster than manual ones, but they also wear down pencils faster. It's most economical to use an automatic one for inexpensive pencils and a manual sharpener for expensive ones.

ERASERS Some erasers can smear, bend, and even tear your paper, so get a good one that erases cleanly without smudges. Kneaded erasers are pliable and can be molded for precise erasing. They leave no residue, and they last a long time.

PENS If you want to outline a drawing after sketching it, you can use a regular Sharpie® pen or marker. For more intricate pieces, try Micron® pens, which come in a variety of tip thicknesses.

DRAWING BASICS

How to Draw Shapes

For the first steps of each project in this book, you will be drawing basic shapes as guide lines. Use light, smooth strokes and don't press down too hard with your pencil. If you sketch lightly at first, it will be easier to erase if you make a mistake.

You'll be drawing a lot of circles, which many beginning artists find difficult to create. These circles do not have to be perfect because they are just guides, but if you want to practice making better circles, try the four-marks method, as shown below.

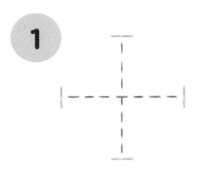

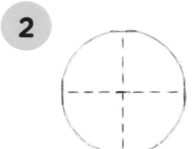

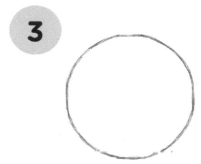

1 Mark where you want the top of the circle and, directly below, make another mark for the bottom. Do the same for the sides of the circle. If it helps, lightly draw a dotted line to help you place the other mark.

2 Once you have the four marks spaced apart equally, connect them using curved lines.

3 Erase any dotted lines you created, and you have a circle!

ADDITIONAL SHAPES While circles are usually what people find the most challenging, there are many other lines and shapes that you should practice and master. An arc can become a muzzle or tongue. Triangles can be ears, teeth, or claws. A football shape can become an eye. A curvy line can make a tail and an angled line a leg. Study the animal and note the shapes that stand out to you.

How to Shade

The final step to drawing an animal is to add shading so that it looks three-dimensional, and then adding texture so that it looks furry, feathery, smooth, or scaly. To introduce yourself to shading, follow the steps below.

1

Understand your pencil with a value scale. Using any pencil, start to shade lightly on one side and gradually darken your strokes toward the other side. This value scale will show you how light and dark your pencil can be.

2

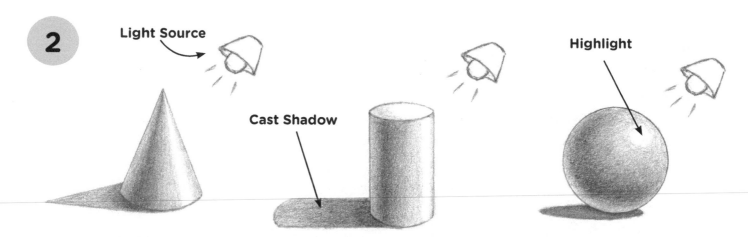

Light Source

Cast Shadow

Highlight

Apply the value scale to simple shapes. Draw simple shapes and shade them to make them look three-dimensional. Observe shadows in real life. Study how the light interacts with simple objects and creates shadows. Then try drawing what you see.

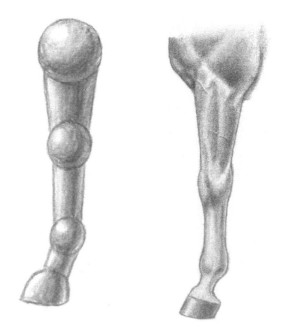

3

Practice with more complex objects. Once you're comfortable shading simple objects, move on to more complex ones. Note, for example, how a horse's leg is made up of cylinders and spheres. Breaking down your subject into simple shapes makes it easier to visualize the shadows.

6

How to Add Texture

Take what you've learned about shading one step further by adding texture to your drawings.

FURRY

One quick pencil stroke creates a single hair. Keep adding more quick, short strokes and you'll get a furry texture. Separate each individual stroke a bit so that the white of the paper comes through.

Create stripes and patterns by varying the pressure on your pencil to get different degrees of tonal value.

Make sure that your strokes follow the forms of the animal. As you shade a furry animal, use strokes that go in the general direction of the fur growth. The fur here follows the form of a simple sphere.

 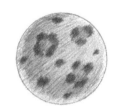

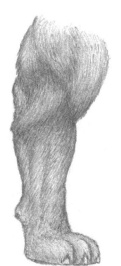

This is how to add fur to a complex form, which is easier if you know the animal's anatomy. In order to show the muscle structure, this image shows an exaggerated example of a lion's front leg and paw.

SMOOTH

For very short fur or smooth skin, add graphite evenly. Blend with a cotton swab, blending stump, or piece of tissue if needed.

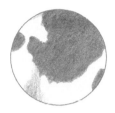

SCALY

For scaly animals like reptiles or dragons, create each individual scale with a tiny arc. Then add shadows to make the form look three-dimensional.

For a much easier way to get a scaly look, just add a bunch of squiggles! Make the squiggles darker in areas of pattern, as well as when adding shadows.

FEATHERED When adding texture to feathered animals, approach it as you would with fur or with smooth skin. Use a series of short strokes for fine or fluffy feathers. For smooth feathers, use even, blended value.

RUBY-THROATED HUMMINGBIRD

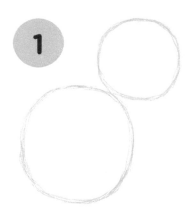

1

Lightly sketch two circles as a guide for the hummingbird's body and head. These circles don't have to be perfect because they're just guide lines.

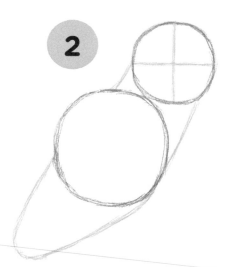

2

Make two intersecting lines inside the head, which will help you place the facial features later on. Then connect the two circles to create the neck and add an arc below the body circle to create the rest of the body.

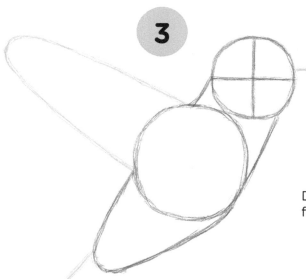

3

Draw a straight line as a guide for beak, an arc for the wings, and a straight line for the tail.

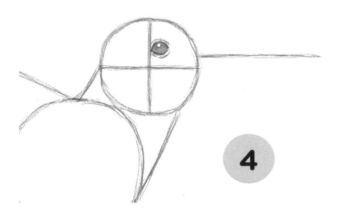

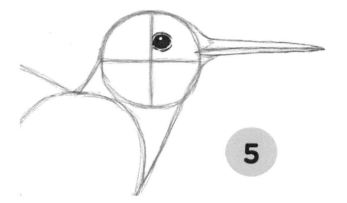

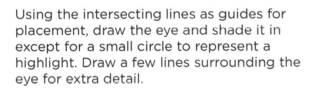

4

Using the intersecting lines as guides for placement, draw the eye and shade it in except for a small circle to represent a highlight. Draw a few lines surrounding the eye for extra detail.

5

Use the line as a guide to draw the long, thin beak. Draw a few quick, short strokes to represent feathers at the base of the beak. Then draw the rest of the head.

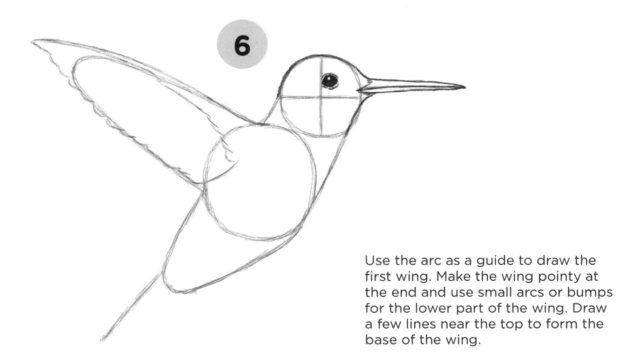

6

Use the arc as a guide to draw the first wing. Make the wing pointy at the end and use small arcs or bumps for the lower part of the wing. Draw a few lines near the top to form the base of the wing.

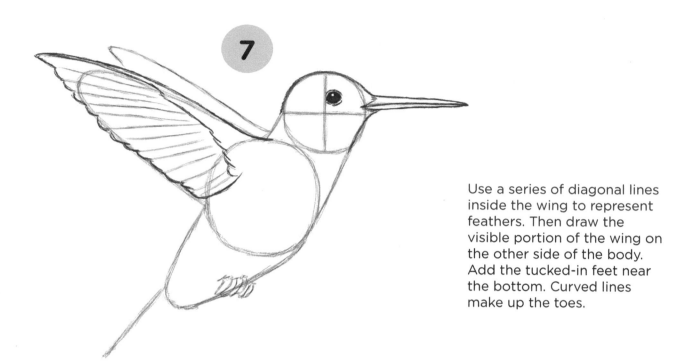

7

Use a series of diagonal lines inside the wing to represent feathers. Then draw the visible portion of the wing on the other side of the body. Add the tucked-in feet near the bottom. Curved lines make up the toes.

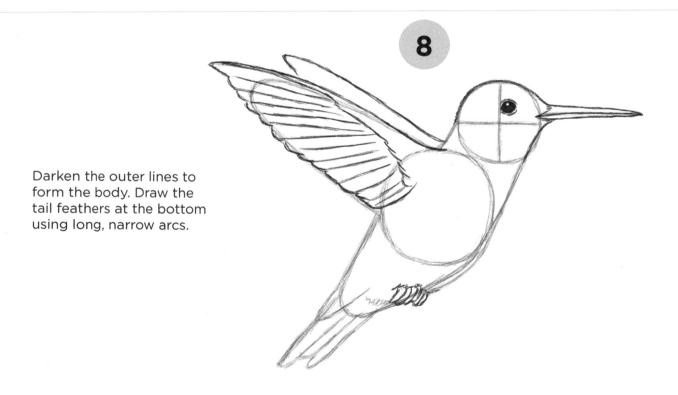

8

Darken the outer lines to form the body. Draw the tail feathers at the bottom using long, narrow arcs.

9

For a cleaner look, erase as much as you can of the initial guide lines. Don't worry about erasing all of them. It's okay to leave some behind. Also re-draw any final sketch lines that you may have accidentally erased.

10

Add some shading to your hummingbird to make it look more three-dimensional. Place a darker value where shadows fall and where the darker feathers are. Shade some small arcs to suggest the ruby-colored feathers found on the throat.

HOUSE SPARROW

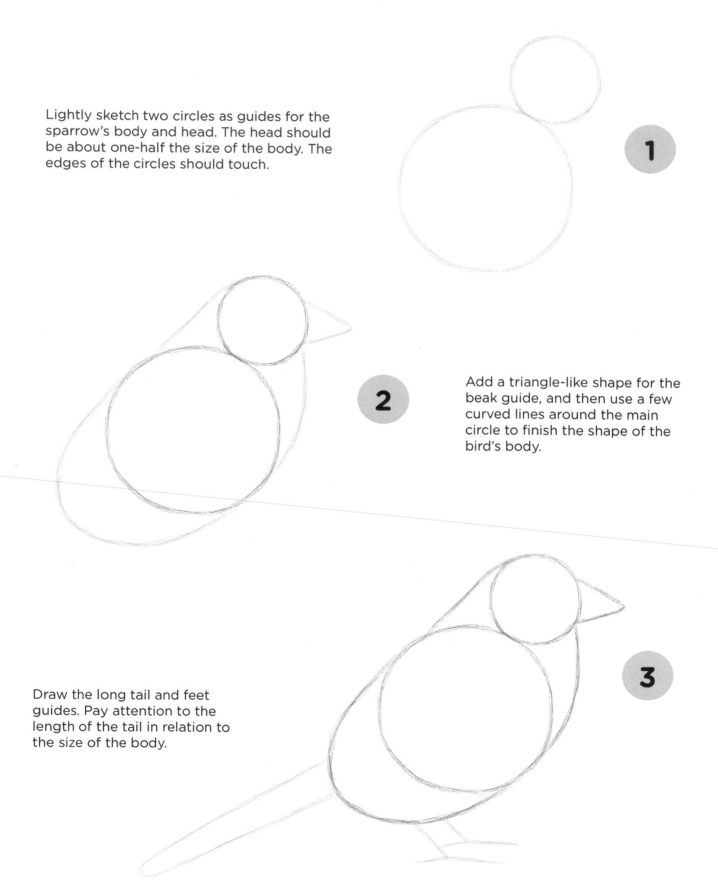

Lightly sketch two circles as guides for the sparrow's body and head. The head should be about one-half the size of the body. The edges of the circles should touch.

1

Add a triangle-like shape for the beak guide, and then use a few curved lines around the main circle to finish the shape of the bird's body.

2

Draw the long tail and feet guides. Pay attention to the length of the tail in relation to the size of the body.

3

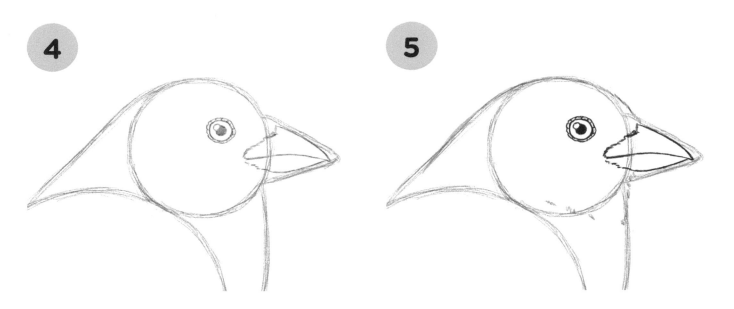

4

Sketch a circle for the eye. Draw a tiny circle for a highlight and add a bigger dot in the middle for the pupil. Draw the beak and add the feathery base with a series of quick, short strokes.

5

Use the initial guides to draw the sparrow's head. Use quick, short strokes under the beak for the bird's feathery throat.

Draw the top part of the wing by first darkening the top, left side of the body. Add a few more detail lines, and then use the guides to draw the front of the body.

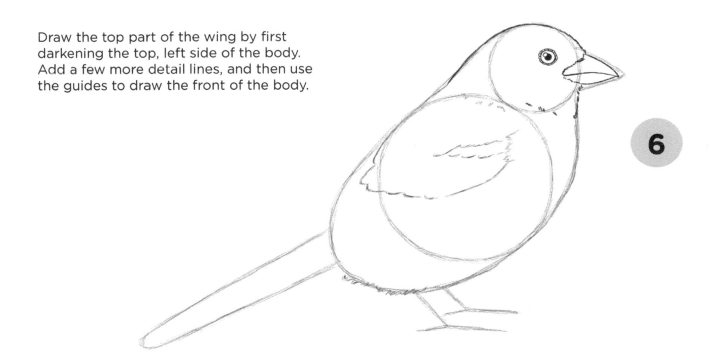

6

7

Finish the wing, and then draw the first foot. Sparrows have one toe pointing backward and three toes pointing forward on each foot. From this angle, the forward-pointing toes will overlap, so only draw the visible parts. On the tip of each toe, draw a sharp claw.

8

Draw the visible parts of the other foot and finish your sketch by adding the tail.

CAST SHADOWS
If a bird isn't flying in your drawing, add a cast shadow underneath it. This will help ground the bird so it doesn't appear to be floating. Use a darker value near the middle of the shadow and a lighter value along the edge.

For a cleaner look, erase as much as you can of the initial guide lines. Don't worry about erasing all of the guides. It's okay to leave some behind. Re-draw any final sketch lines that you may have accidentally erased.

9

Shading will give your sparrow more dimension and volume. Add a dark value to the beak and throat, around the eye and back of the head, in stripes on the wing feathers, and on the claws. Use a lighter value in other areas of the head, on a section of the wing, and on the front of the body. As you add the value, use strokes that go in the general direction of the feathers.

10

MALLARD DUCK

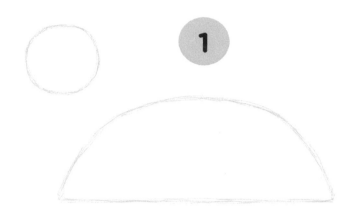

Lightly draw a big half-circle near the bottom of your paper as a guide for the body. Then draw a small circle as guide for the head.

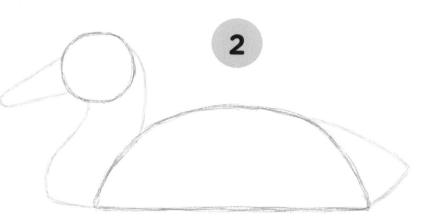

On the lower, left side of the head, draw a sloping arc as a guide for the duck's bill. Add a couple of curved lines that connect the head to the body and draw two curved lines that come to a pointy tip for the tail.

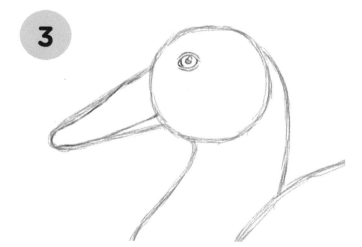

Draw the eye and a couple of curved lines around it for extra detail. Then use the initial arc as a guide to draw the top part of the bill.

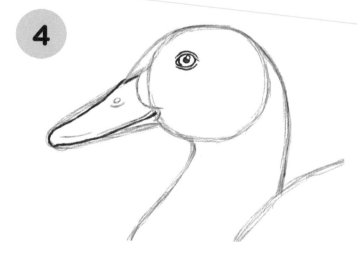

Draw a line along the bottom edge of the bill to create a small ridge. Add the base of the bill, the mouth below, and the nostril. Finish the head by darkening the outer edges of the initial guides.

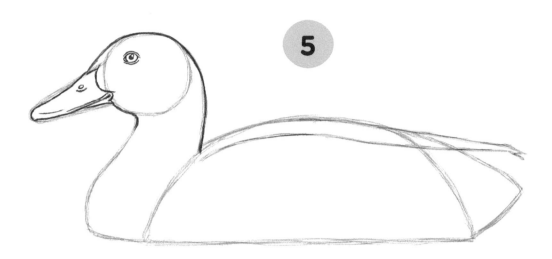

On top of the body, draw two wavy horizontal lines for the tops of the folded wings.

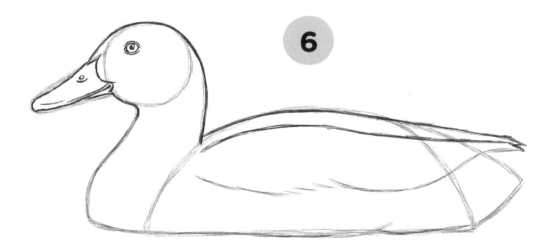

Complete the duck's left wing. The bottom edge should be wavy, and the tip of it should come out of the shape of the body. Use a few broken lines near the middle to represent a few feathers. Then finish the neck and bottom of the body. Leave the tail for the next step.

7

Use the pointy shape on the right as a guide to draw the tail, and add a few more short lines inside the body for detail. Two lines on the bottom of the duck represent the leg that's visible above the water.

8

Add some straight and curved lines around your duck for the water.

Erase guide lines and tidy up your drawing.

Note where the lightest and darkest values are on this drawing. Leave the shine in the eye, the neck band, and some areas on and around the tail white. The tip of the beak, head, rear feathers, and area of water that's closest to the bird's body are the darkest. Smooth shading gives the appearance of shiny feathers, so take your time to get this texture. As you shade the water, note how the mallard's head creates a shadow on it. The ripples on the water are also of lighter and darker values.

TIGER SWALLOWTAIL BUTTERFLY

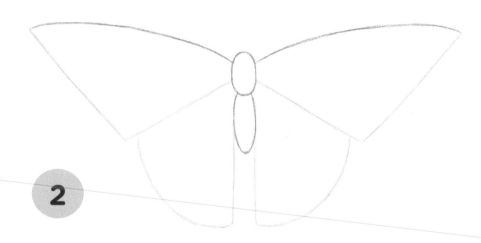

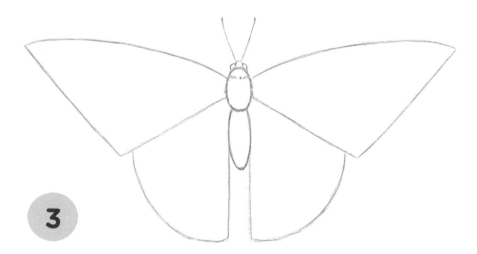

1 Lightly sketch a small oval for the thorax. Below that, draw a longer oval for the abdomen. Then make curved lines for the tops of the wings. Pay attention to the length of these lines in relation to the body and make sure they have the same length and curvature.

2 Complete the forewings with angled lines. Under the abdomen, draw two vertical, parallel lines for the first part of the hindwings. Then, on either side, draw a curved line that ends near where the forewings bend. Make sure the wings look symmetrical before moving on to the next step.

3 On top of the first oval, draw a small arc for the tip of the butterfly's head and add small, curved lines on either side for the eyes. Darken the two body ovals and use a series of short strokes for a fuzzy texture. Add two long lines for the antennae, making the tips a bit thicker.

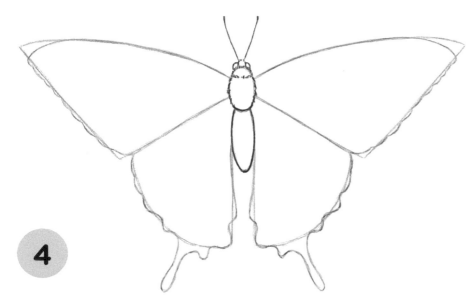

Draw the forewings on top, making the tips curvier and the sides wavier than the guide lines. Then complete the hindwings using wavy lines. At the bottom, draw a thin, long shape to give the wing the "swallowtail" look. Make the wings look the same on each side so that your butterfly is symmetrical.

4

SYMMETRY Everything on this butterfly's wings is symmetrical. It might be a challenge to draw everything on the right side as the mirror image of what you drew on the left, so draw very lightly at first and don't be afraid to use your eraser! Don't worry too much about being perfect, though. Just have fun drawing it.

In this step and the next, add the vein lines. The pattern will come later.

5

Sketch in a series of sloping lines on the forewings for the rest of the veins.

6

Now begin adding the pattern with wavy lines, making sure not to draw these pattern lines too close to the edge.

7

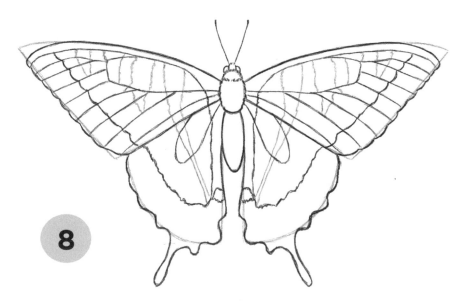

For an organic feel, the "tiger" stripes in this step shouldn't be made with perfectly straight lines. Instead use quick, short pencil strokes. On each wing, add one long stripe that reaches down into the hindwings, and three short stripes on the forewings. All of these stripes should overlap the veins.

8

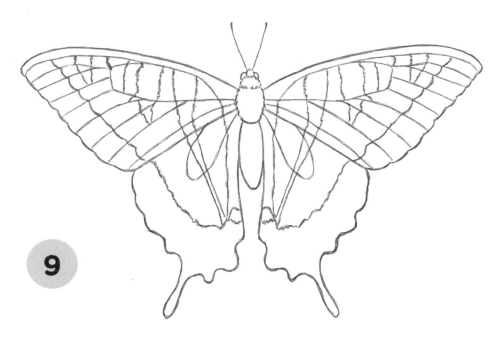

9

Clean up your drawing by erasing guide lines and re-drawing anything you'd like. Fix any details on the wings that don't look symmetrical.

10

Shade your butterfly drawing! Use light value where the yellow portions of the butterfly are, a middle value where the blue would be (the bottoms of the hindwings), and a dark value for the black stripes. As you add black to the outer parts of the wings, leave lighter circles for additional detail on the pattern. Push lightly with your pencil at first and slowly build up the darker value. The body should also be black except for the outer edges.

EMPEROR PENGUIN

1 Sketch three circles as guides for the body and head. Pay attention to the sizes and placement of the circles. If the guides are drawn correctly now, your penguin won't end up looking too short or tall or thin or fat. It will look just right.

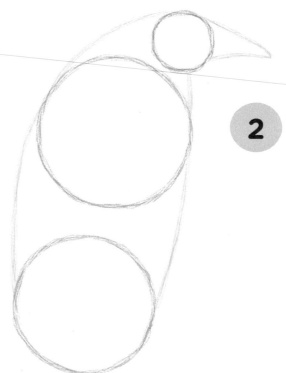

2 Connect the circles with curved lines to form the body and add a triangle shape as a guide for the beak.

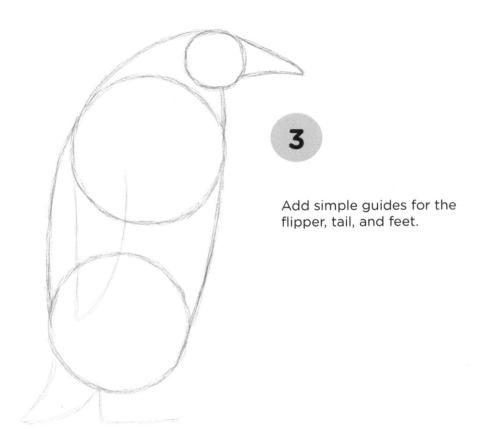

3

Add simple guides for the flipper, tail, and feet.

4

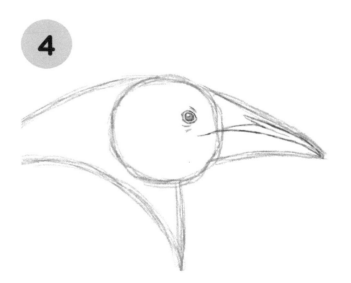

Draw the penguin's eye and add a few lines around it for extra detail. Shade in the eyeball completely except for the highlight. Then, using the triangle as a guide, begin on the beak.

5

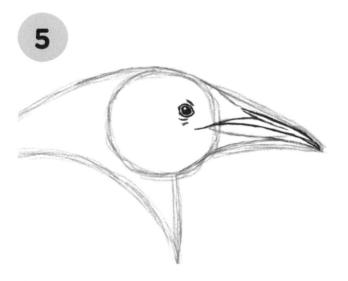

Finish the bottom of the beak, and then complete the head using the initial shapes as guides.

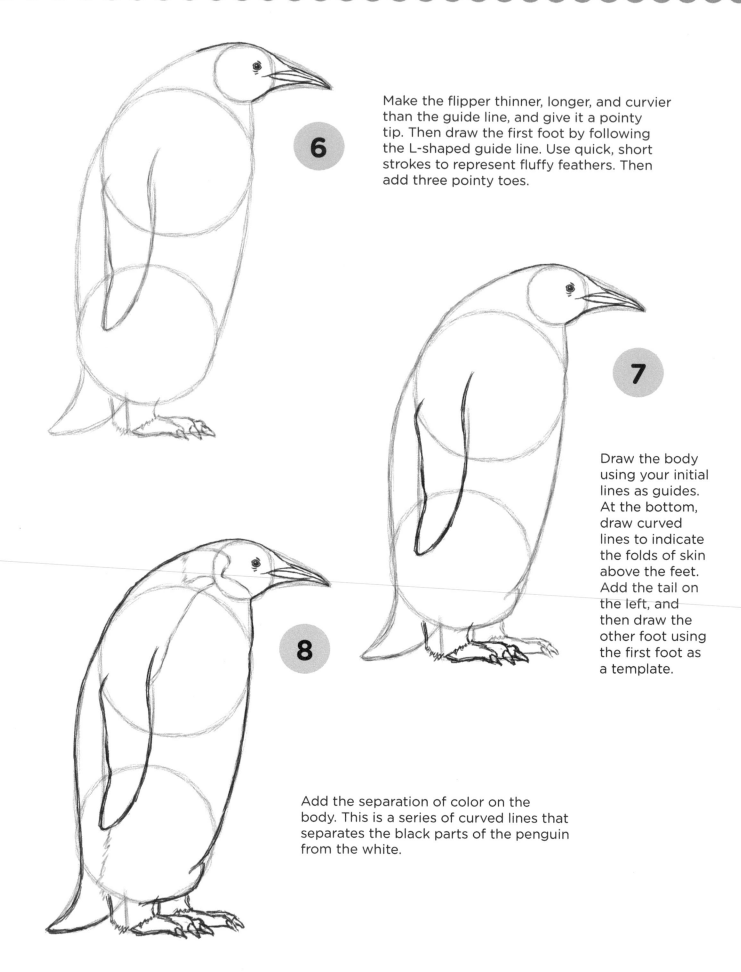

6 Make the flipper thinner, longer, and curvier than the guide line, and give it a pointy tip. Then draw the first foot by following the L-shaped guide line. Use quick, short strokes to represent fluffy feathers. Then add three pointy toes.

7 Draw the body using your initial lines as guides. At the bottom, draw curved lines to indicate the folds of skin above the feet. Add the tail on the left, and then draw the other foot using the first foot as a template.

8 Add the separation of color on the body. This is a series of curved lines that separates the black parts of the penguin from the white.

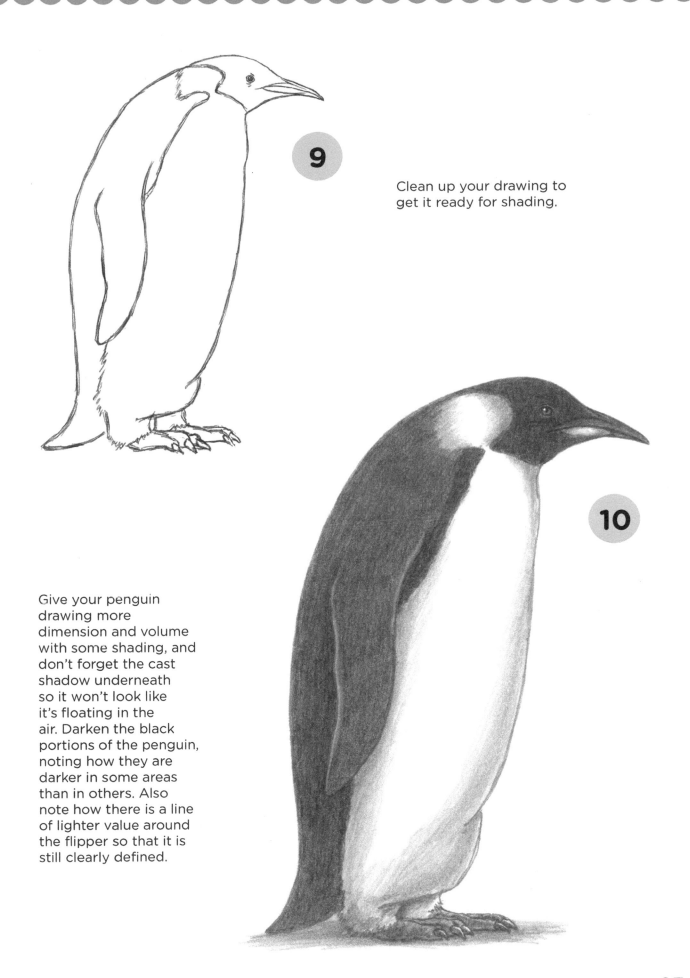

9

Clean up your drawing to get it ready for shading.

10

Give your penguin drawing more dimension and volume with some shading, and don't forget the cast shadow underneath so it won't look like it's floating in the air. Darken the black portions of the penguin, noting how they are darker in some areas than in others. Also note how there is a line of lighter value around the flipper so that it is still clearly defined.

DOVE

Draw two circles on your page, leaving enough room for the wings.

1

Connect the head and body circles to create the neck. Add the bottom part of the body as an arc, a triangular shape for the beak, and two lines to start the wings. Bend the lines near the middle to indicate the joints, and make the line on the right shorter.

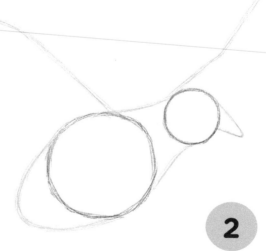

2

3 Finish up your guide lines by completing the wing shapes, adding the tail guide, and couple of lines for the feet.

GUIDE LINES Remember to sketch in guide lines lightly, and don't worry if your shapes aren't perfect. Instead of worrying about making a perfect circle, for example, focus more on the size and placement of each shape in relation to the rest.

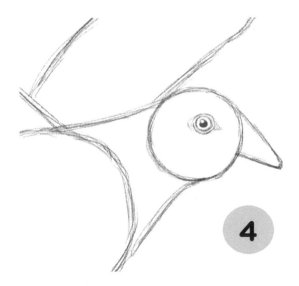

4 Draw the eye as a small circle. Add a dark pupil and a white highlight circle inside. Draw a few lines surrounding the eye for extra detail.

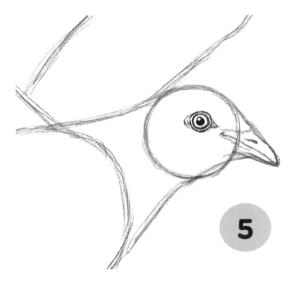

5 Use the triangle-like shape as a guide to draw the beak. Use quick, short strokes for the base of the beak, and add a small slit at the top for the nostril. Then use the original circle as a guide to draw the rest of the head.

Follow the path of the guides as you darken the wings. Draw the bottoms with curved lines, which represent the feathers. The curves should get smaller and closer together as they get closer to the body.

6

Draw lines in the wings for further structure and extra detail. Then use the small lines underneath the body to draw the feet.

7

Darken the sides of the tail and add a few straight lines within the shape for the tail feathers. Then darken the remaining guide lines to complete the body.

8

Tidy up your pencil lines and stop here for a nice sketch of a white dove, or move on to the next step to add shading.

9

10

Even though this is a white dove, you can make it look more three-dimensional with shading. Pick the direction of the light source when shading so that the shadows are consistent. Since the light source is coming from the top-right, shade where the shadows should be, including on the underside of the body and wings.

BALD EAGLE

1

Draw two circles and an arc as a guide for the bald eagle's body and head.

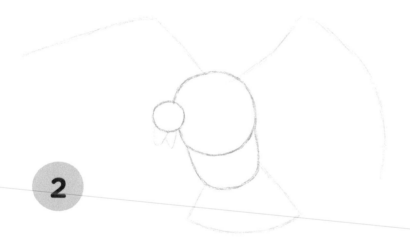

2

Add guides for the open beak and tail, and carefully place the guides for the tops of the outstretched wings.

3

Finish up your guides by connecting the head to the body to form the neck, adding leg guides, and completing the wing guides. Note how the wings are not symmetrical.

4

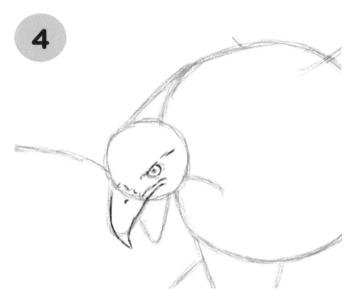

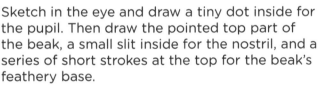

Sketch in the eye and draw a tiny dot inside for the pupil. Then draw the pointed top part of the beak, a small slit inside for the nostril, and a series of short strokes at the top for the beak's feathery base.

5

Finish the bottom part of the beak, adding the tongue inside the open mouth. Then darken the head and neck. To the right of the head, inside the body, draw a series of short strokes for the feathers at the bottom of the neck.

6

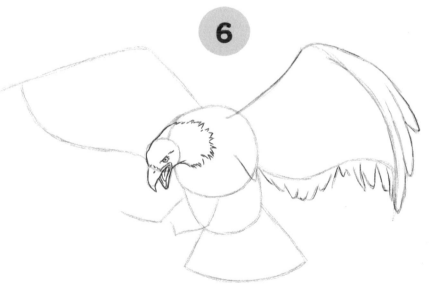

Darken the guide for the wing, adding three additional long arcs for feathers on the right side. Finish the bottom of the wing with a series of small arcs to create the feathers.

7

Now draw the other wing, adding a series of thin, long arcs along the bottom for the feathers. Along the top, draw a curved line to emphasize the curve of the bird's wing.

Carefully add the eagle's talon, with three toes and claws in the front and one in the back. Then draw the feathered leg with quick pencil strokes to add the fluffy texture.

8

Draw the other foot and leg the same way. This foot is at a different angle from the first foot, so the toes should look more spread out.

9

Draw a series of short strokes along the bottom of the body to indicate where the tail starts. Then follow the path of the bottom line and draw a series of small arcs for tail feathers. Give the feathers varying thicknesses and add some different-sized gaps between the feathers.

10

For a cleaner look, erase guide lines and re-draw anything you'd like before you start to shade.

Use a dark value everywhere except the head, tail, and feet. As you shade, use strokes that go in the general direction of the feathers. Don't worry about shading too smoothly. The rough value will give the feathers some texture. Use a slightly lighter value in the wings for the rows of feathers and along the top edges of the wings. Finally, add some shadows to the white sections to give the figure more dimension and volume.

MONARCH BUTTERFLY

1

Draw a big shape as a guide for the butterfly's hindwing.

2

On top of the hindwing, draw the shape of the forewing.

3

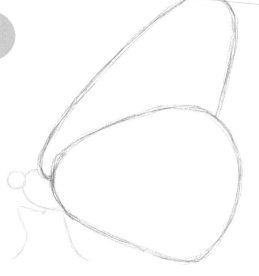

On the left side, draw an arc and a small circle for the body and head. Two lines make up the leg guides.

4

Finish up your guides with two curved lines in the hindwing and two in the forewing.

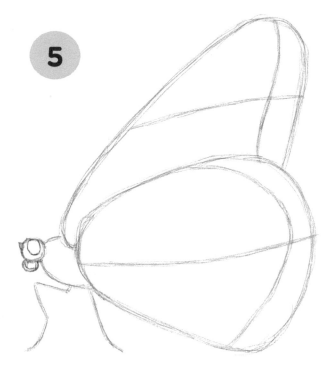

5

Add the eye, which is almost as big as the head, and then draw a series of short strokes along the path of the small circle to create the fuzzy head. Several small, curved lines under the head create the monarch's rolled-up proboscis.

6

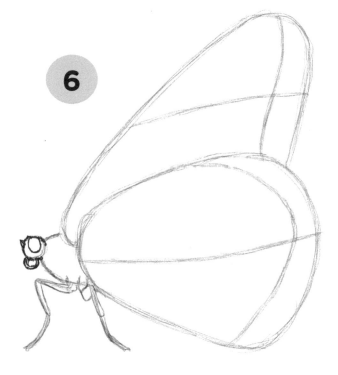

Use the angled lines under the body to draw the thin legs. Make sure the tips of both legs are on the same level. Then draw a series of short strokes along the guide in the middle for the fuzzy thorax.

7

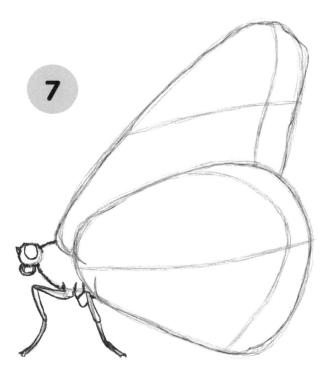

Use the big shapes on the right to draw the butterfly's wings with wavy lines for an organic look. Note how the hindwing attaches to the body on the left side.

8

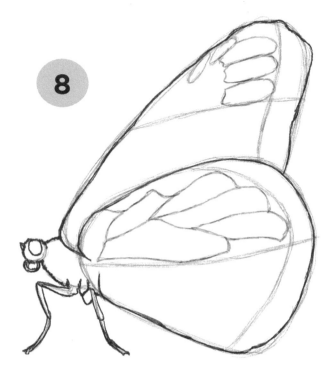

Begin to add the detail inside the wings with long shapes. Pay close attention to the reference image when drawing these shapes. You will add the rest of the pattern (the white spots) when you shade in the last step.

Continue adding shapes made up of curved lines. Use the initial lines as guides for placement.

9

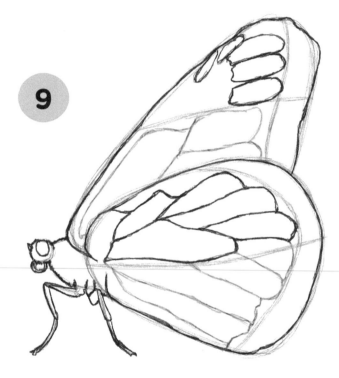

10

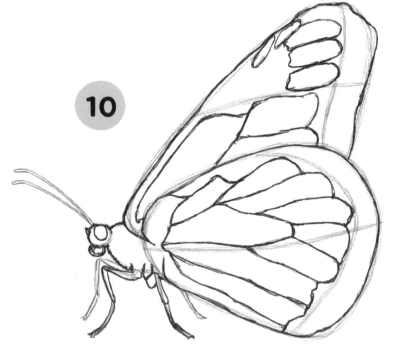

On top of the head, draw two long lines that curve to the left for the antennae. Make the tips slightly thicker. Then use the first set of legs as templates to draw the visible legs on the other side the same way. The last set of hind legs are hidden behind the wings.

11

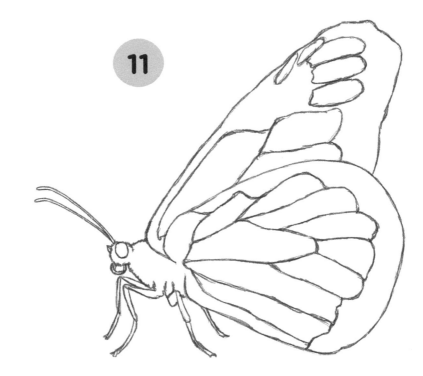

Erase guide lines and tidy up your drawing.

12

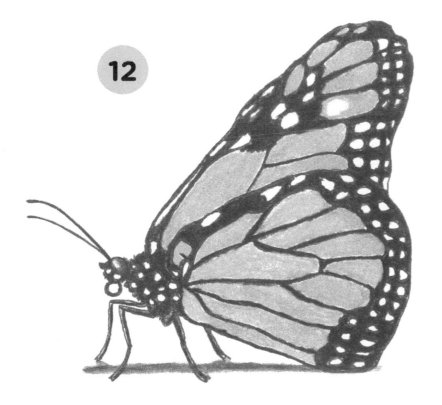

As you shade the outer edges of the wings and in the body, leave a lot of little areas white. The spots along the right side should be somewhat arranged into two columns, and the ones near the top edge of each wing should be slightly bigger. Add dark value to the veins and make the lines a bit thicker. Add a light-to-medium value to the inside of the wings. Because the butterfly is standing and not flying, add a cast shadow underneath.

NOTING DIFFERENCES While all butterflies have a similar structure, there are noticeable differences between the different kinds. How does this butterfly differ from the tiger swallowtail starting on page 20? Could you draw the swallowtail in this pose and the monarch in the swallowtail's pose? What other information would you need to know before trying? (For example, you would need to research what a swallowtail's legs look like, what a monarch's wingspan looks like, etc.)

ROOSTER

1

Lightly sketch two circles, taking note of their sizes and placement in relation to each other. Roosters have small heads, so draw the head very small.

2

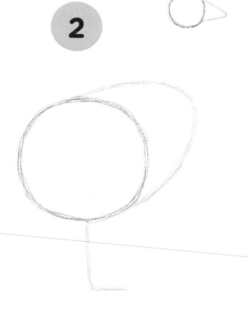

Draw a triangle-like shape coming off of the head circle. Then add an arc on the upper right side of the circle to finish up the guide for the rooster's body. The end result should be a shape similar to an egg. Also make an L-shaped line for the feet.

3

With a couple of curved lines, connect the head and body to form the neck. Then draw a long, curved line on the left side of the body as a guide for the rooster's showy tail.

4

Draw the eye and a couple of curved lines around it for extra detail. Then use the triangle shape to draw the curved beak that points down at the tip. Draw a small teardrop shape for the nostril.

5

Draw the crest or comb on top of the head with two curved lines and wavy spikes in between. Draw the spikes at different lengths and thicknesses, with the longer ones in the middle. Add short strokes for the fine feathers on top of the head.

6

Draw the loose skin under the beak, which is called a wattle. Draw a wavy curve around the eye for the fleshy part inside the head and add a few additional short strokes for more detail.

7

Draw the rest of the head and neck. Then, using quick, short strokes, add some of the fine feather tips along the bottom of the neck and the rump.

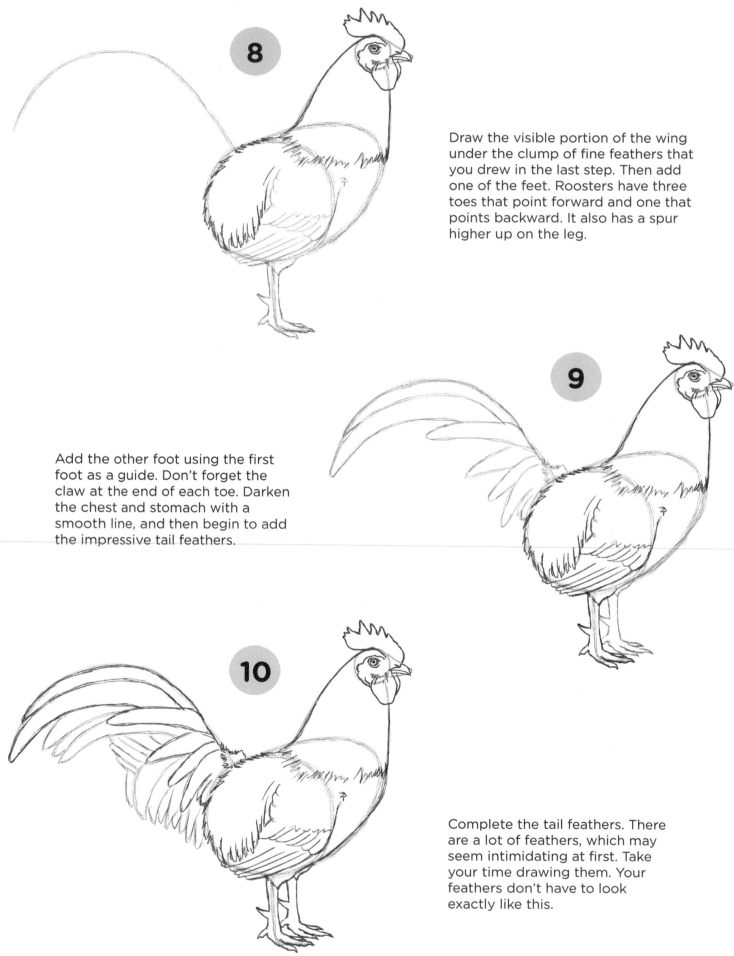

8

Draw the visible portion of the wing under the clump of fine feathers that you drew in the last step. Then add one of the feet. Roosters have three toes that point forward and one that points backward. It also has a spur higher up on the leg.

Add the other foot using the first foot as a guide. Don't forget the claw at the end of each toe. Darken the chest and stomach with a smooth line, and then begin to add the impressive tail feathers.

9

10

Complete the tail feathers. There are a lot of feathers, which may seem intimidating at first. Take your time drawing them. Your feathers don't have to look exactly like this.

11

Erase as much as you can of the initial guide lines and re-draw anything you'd like to fix.

12

Add some shading to your rooster and add a cast shadow underneath so it doesn't appear to be floating. Note the areas of dark value in this drawing, and where the lighter creates a sleek and shiny look.

BARN OWL

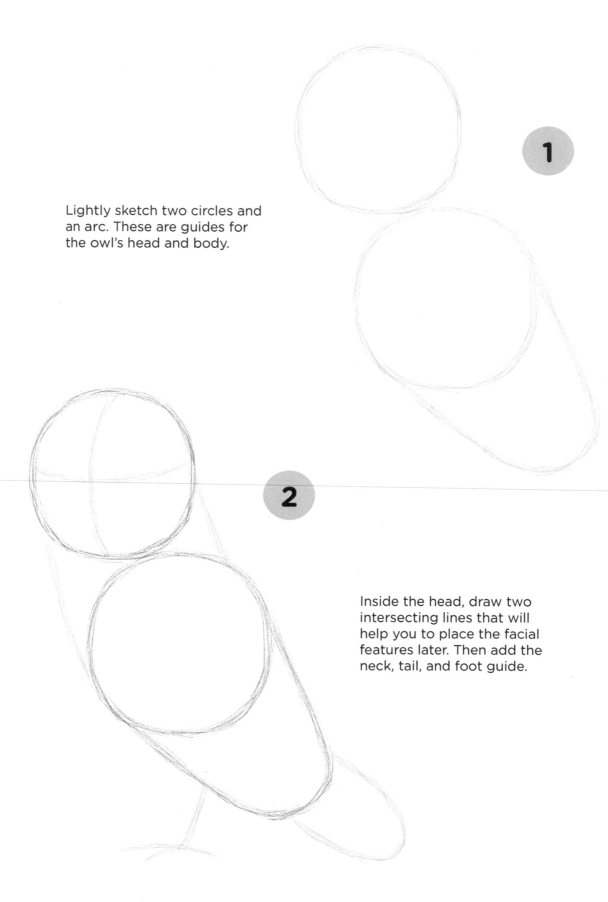

Lightly sketch two circles and an arc. These are guides for the owl's head and body.

Inside the head, draw two intersecting lines that will help you to place the facial features later. Then add the neck, tail, and foot guide.

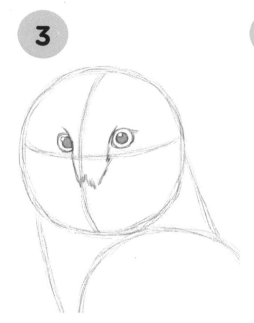

Draw the eyes using the guides for placement. The eye on the left should be slightly smaller due to perspective. Then add the feathers that cover the top part of the beak.

For the beak, draw a small, V-shaped line under the feathers. Then complete the heart-shaped face using quick, short strokes.

Add another layer around the heart-like shape by adding darker, curvier lines on the outside. Then complete the head using the main circle as a guide.

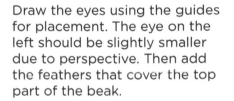

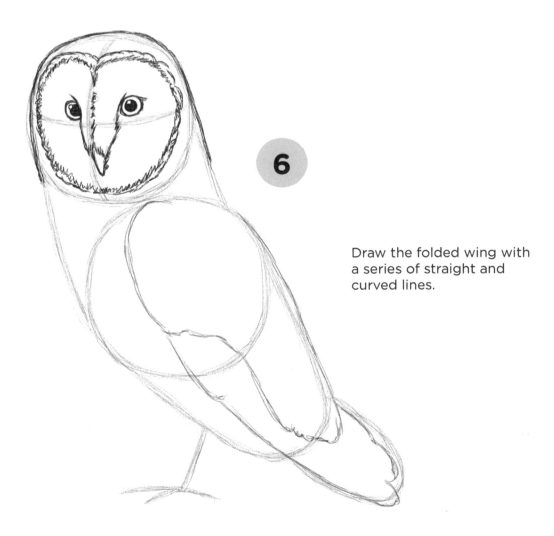

Draw the folded wing with a series of straight and curved lines.

After adding lines and some curves inside the wing to suggest the feathers, draw the first foot. Make the leg thick and use quick, short strokes for the feathers at the top. At the end of each toe, draw a talon.

HIDDEN ANATOMY While owls have four toes, only draw the toes that are visible from the angle you are viewing the owl. When drawing, it helps if you are familiar with the animal's anatomy, but it isn't absolutely necessary if you make sure to observe your subject really well.

Draw the visible portion of the other leg. Then complete the rest of the body using the remaining lines as guides. Make sure to draw the short tail feathers at the bottom and add a hint of the other wing on the other side of the body.

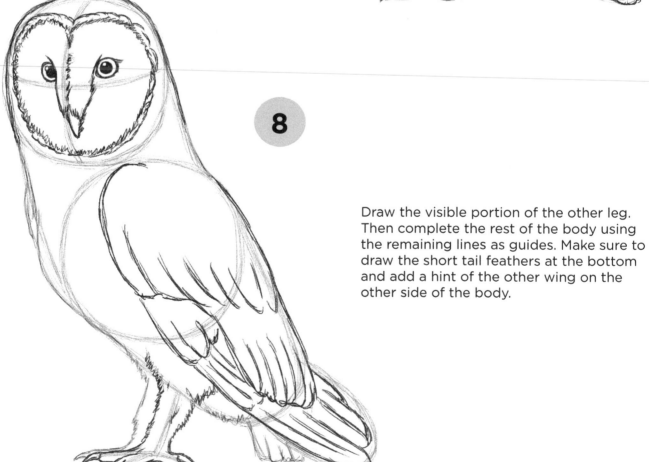

For a cleaner look, erase as much as you can of the initial guide lines and re-draw anything you'd like.

9

10

Add some shading to your drawing, keeping in mind where shadows should fall, including under the folded wing, on the chest, and on the ground where the owl casts a shadow. As you add value to the backside of the body, draw some speckles throughout the wing and body for further detail.

ABOUT THE AUTHOR

How2DrawAnimals.com teaches beginning artists how to draw all kinds of animals from A to Z through video demonstrations and simple step-by-step instructions. Started in 2012 by an animal-loving artist with a bachelor's degree in illustration, How2DrawAnimals offers a new tutorial each week and now boasts hundreds of animal drawing tutorials. Working in graphite and in colored pencils, and in both realistic and cartoon styles, How2DrawAnimals has featured animals from all letters of the alphabet, from Aardvark to Zebra and everything in between. See more at How2DrawAnimals.com.

ALSO IN THE LET'S DRAW SERIES:

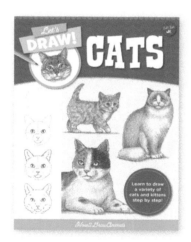

Let's Draw Cats
ISBN: 978-0-7603-8070-3

Let's Draw Dogs
ISBN: 978-0-7603-8072-7

Let's Draw Favorite Animals
ISBN: 978-0-7603-8074-1

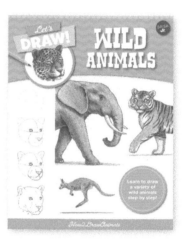

Let's Draw Wild Animals
ISBN: 978-0-7603-8076-5

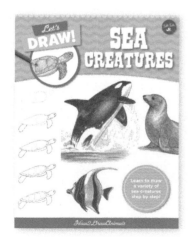

Let's Draw Sea Creatures
ISBN: 978-0-7603-8080-2

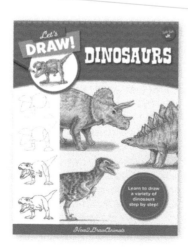

Let's Draw Dinosaurs
ISBN: 978-0-7603-8082-6

Let's Draw Dragons
ISBN: 978-0-7603-8084-0

The Quarto Group

Inspiring | Educating | Creating | Entertaining

www.WalterFoster.com

CPSIA information can be obtained
at www.ICGtesting.com
Printed in the USA
JSHW061207181122
33414JS00004B/8